Jin and the Rat!

By Cameron Macintosh

Jin the cub can see a rat!

The rat can see Jin.

The rat runs into a pit.

Run, run, run!

Jin runs to the pit.

He tips into it!

Bop, bop, bop!

Jin sits up.

Jin can not jog up.

Jin digs in the mud.

Dig, dig, dig!

Up, up, up!

Jin gets to the top of the pit.

He has a nap!

CHECKING FOR MEANING

1. Where did the rat run? *(Literal)*

2. How did Jin get into the pit? *(Literal)*

3. How did Jin get out of the pit? *(Inferential)*

EXTENDING VOCABULARY

runs	Explain that *runs* is a word that describes the action of the rat and Jin in the story. Find the words *digs* and *gets*, two other action words.
bop	What does *bop* mean? Why is this word in the text? Explain that the word *bop* is the sound of Jin falling into the pit.
top	Say the sounds in the word *top*. Can you make another word using the same three letters?

MOVING BEYOND THE TEXT

1. What are some places small animals hide so they don't get caught by other animals?

2. Which animals might try to catch a rat for food?

3. Do you think Jin was clever to get out of the pit? Why?

4. Where do you think the rat went?

SPEED SOUNDS

Dd	Jj	Oo	Gg	Uu

Cc	Bb	Rr	Ee	Ff	Hh	Nn

Mm	Ss	Aa	Pp	Ii	Tt

PRACTICE WORDS

cub

runs

Jin

up

not

bop

Bop

mud

jog

digs

on

gets

top